Social Studies Alive!™
My School and Family

Teachers' Curriculum Institute

Bert Bower   Jim Lobdell

Managing Editor: Laura M. Alavosus
Project Editor: Wendy Frey
Production Editor: Mali Apple
Editorial Assistant: Anna Embree
Art Director: Tim Stephenson
Production Coordinator: Lynn Sanchez
Senior Graphic Designer: Christy Uyeno
Graphic Designers: Katy Haun, Victoria Philp,
    Paul Rebello
Photographer: Tim Stephenson
Photo Acquisitions: Anna Embree
Audio Director: Katy Haun
Operations Manager: Ellen Mapstone

This book is published by Teachers' Curriculum Institute.

Teachers' Curriculum Institute
PO Box 50996
Palo Alto, CA 94303

Customer Service: 800-497-6138
www.socialstudiesalive.net

ISBN 1-58371-251-8
2 3 4 5 6 7 8 9 10 07 06 05 04

Program Directors

Bert Bower

Jim Lobdell

Program Author

Vicki LaBoskey, Professor of Education,

Mills College, Oakland, California

Ph.D., Curriculum and Teacher Education,

Stanford University, Stanford, California

Student Edition/Big Book Authors

Laura M. Alavosus

Wendy Frey

Curriculum Developers

Joyce Bartky

Nicolle Hutchinson

Reading Specialist

Barbara Schubert, Reading Specialist,

Saint Mary's College, Moraga, California

Ph.D., Education: International Studies,

University of Santa Barbara, Santa Barbara,

California

Teacher Consultants

Jill Bartky, Elementary Teacher,

Sharp Park Elementary School, Pacifica,

California

Debra Elsen, Elementary Teacher,

Manchester Elementary, Manchester, Maryland

Patrick J. Lee, Elementary Teacher,

Ohlone Elementary, Palo Alto, California

Jennifer Miley, Elementary Teacher,

Duveneck Elementary School,

Palo Alto, California

Jodi Perraud, Elementary Teacher,

Boulevard Heights Elementary,

Hollywood, Florida

Internet and Literature Consultant

Debra Elsen, Elementary Teacher,

Manchester Elementary, Manchester, Maryland

Music Specialist

Beth Yankee, Elementary Teacher,

The Woodward School for Technology and

Research, Kalamazoo, Michigan

Geography Specialist

David Knipfer

Mapping Specialists, Ltd.

Madison, Wisconsin

Contents

Chapter 1

How Do We Get Along in School? 2

We share. We talk. We listen.
We take turns.

Chapter 2

Why Is It Important to Learn from Each Other? 8

Each of us is special.
We are good at different things.

Chapter 3

Why Do Schools Have Rules? 14

We need to get along. We need to be safe. We need to be fair. We need to learn.

Chapter 4

Who Helps Us at School? . . 20

Teachers help us at school.

The principal helps us at school.

Chapter 5

How Are We Good Helpers
at School? 26

We help others. We take care of our things. We do our best. We respect others.

Chapter 6

What Is a Map? 32

A map is a drawing of a place.

A map has symbols. A map has a key.

Chapter 7

What Was School Like
Long Ago? 38

Schoolhouses were different.

Classrooms were different.

Chapter 8

What Groups Do
We Belong To? 44

We belong to school groups.

We belong to family groups.

We belong to community groups.

Chapter 9

How Are Families Special? . 50

Families have different members.

Families live in different homes.

Families like different activities.

Chapter 10

What Do Families Need
and Want? 56

Families need food. Families need

clothing. Families need shelter.

Chapter 11

How Do Family Members Care for Each Other? 62

Family members help each other with chores. Family members share what they know.

Chapter 12

How Do Families Change? . 68

Families change over time. Family members grow older.

Chapter 13

What Are Family Traditions? 74

Traditions are special ways of doing things.

Chapter 14

What Do Good Neighbors Do? 80

Good neighbors help each other. Good neighbors get along.

Credits 86

How Do We Get Along in School?

New Ideas

share

talk

listen

take turns

We Share

We get along by sharing.

We share because we often like

to do the same things.

It feels good to share with our friends!

What do we share?

We Talk

We get along by talking.

Talking about our feelings helps

others understand us.

When we understand each other,

we can get along better.

When do we talk to others?

We Listen

We get along by listening.

We listen to our friends' feelings.

We listen to our friends' ideas.

We listen to our teacher.

How do we listen?

We Take Turns

We get along by taking turns. When we take turns, we each get to do something we like to do. When do we take turns?

Wrap-Up

We get along by sharing, talking, listening, and taking turns.

What else can we do to get along?

Why Is It Important to Learn from Each Other?

New Ideas

alike

different

learn

Each of Us Is Special

We are all alike in some ways.

We are different in some ways, too.

Each of us is special.

What makes you special?

We Are Good at Different Things

Some of us are good at drawing.

Some of us are good at counting.

Some of us are good at singing.

What things can you do well?

You Can Learn from Me

I can help you learn new things.

I can catch a baseball.

I can do magic tricks.

What would you like to learn from me?

I Can Learn from You

You can help me learn new things.

I want to learn how to play the drums.

I want to learn how to make a puppet.

What would you like to help me learn?

Wrap-Up

Each of us is special.

We are good at different things.

You can learn from me.

I can learn from you.

13

Why Do Schools Have Rules?

New Ideas

get along

be safe

be fair

learn

Rules Help Us Get Along

We need to get along at school.

We are kind.

We talk and listen to each other.

What else do we do to get along

at school?

16

Rules Help Us Be Safe

We need to be safe at school.

We line up.

We don't run.

What else do we do to be safe

at school?

Rules Help Us Be Fair

We need to be fair at school.

We share.

We take turns.

What else do we do to be fair at school?

Rules Help Us Learn

We need to learn at school.

We pay attention.

We do our schoolwork.

What else do we do to learn at school?

Wrap-Up

We need to get along.

We need to be safe.

We need to be fair.

We need to learn.

Who Helps Us at School?

New Ideas

teacher

principal

secretary

custodian

A Teacher

I like to help children learn.

I like to learn, too.

I listen to children.

I teach children new things.

Who am I?

A Principal

I am a leader.

I like to help teachers and students.

I like to help families.

I am proud of my school.

Who am I?

A Secretary

I like to greet visitors.

I like to help the principal.

I answer the telephone.

I answer questions.

Who am I?

A Custodian

I like to keep our school clean.

I like to fix things.

Sometimes I work outdoors.

I keep our school safe.

Who am I?

Wrap-Up

Teachers help us at school.

The principal helps us at school.

The secretary helps us at school.

The custodian helps us at school.

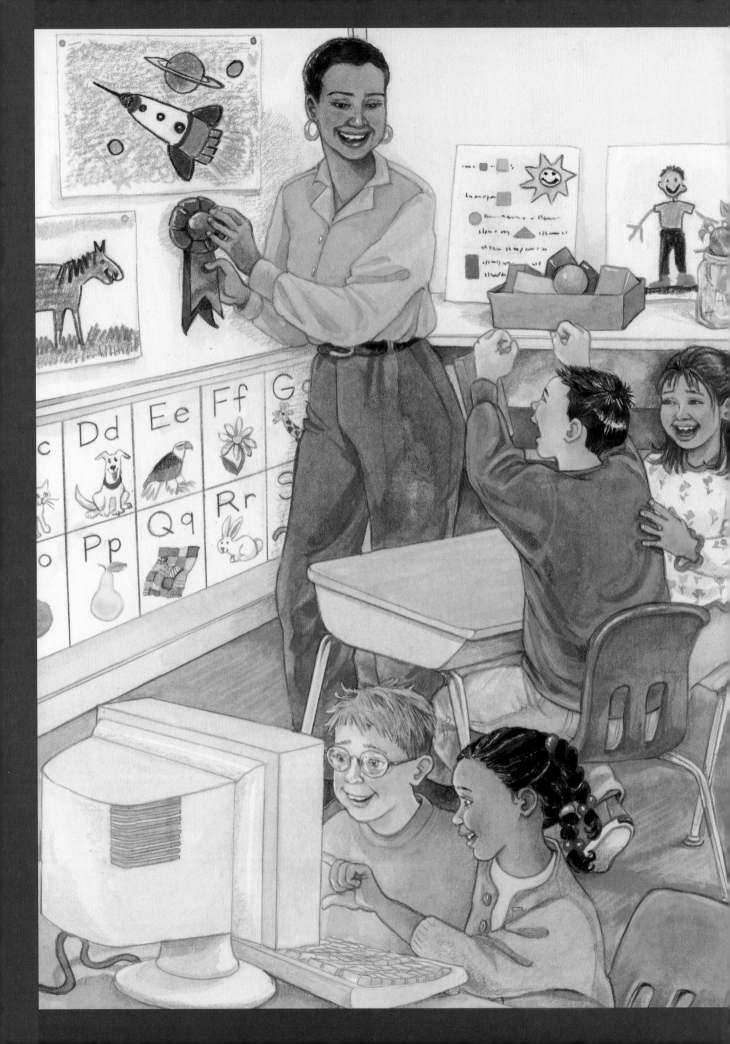

How Are We Good Helpers at School?

New Ideas

help others

take care of our

things

do our best

respect others

We Help Others

We help others at school.

We help the teacher clean up.

We share books with friends.

How else do we help each other?

We Take Care of Our Things

We take care of our things at school.

We are careful with our crayons.

We put our balls away after recess.

How else do we take care of our things at school?

We Do Our Best

We do our best at school.

We ask questions.

We remember to line up for recess.

How else do we do our best at school?

We Respect Others

We respect others at school.

We say "Please" and "Thank you."

We are good winners and losers.

How else do we respect others at school?

Wrap-Up

We help others.

We take care of our things.

We do our best.

We respect others.

What Is a Map?

New Ideas

map

symbol

map key

direction

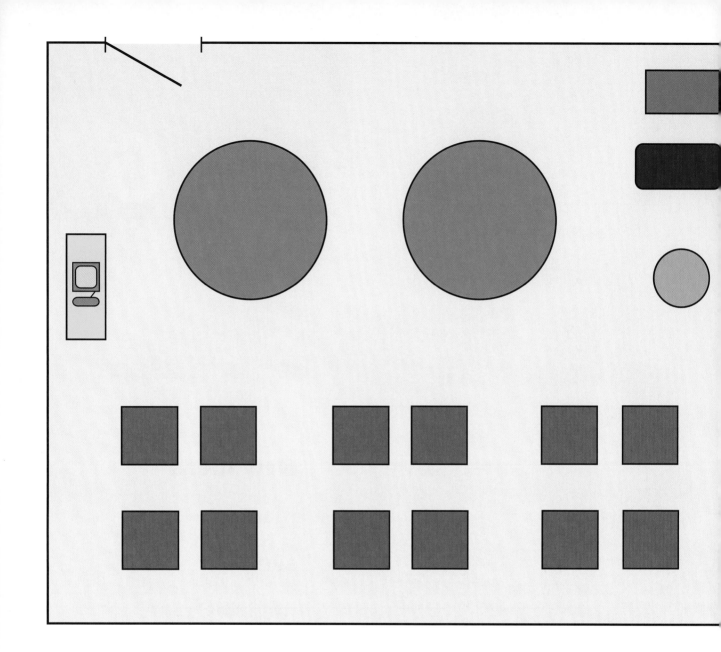

A Map Is a Drawing of a Place

Some maps show countries.

Some maps show cities.

Some maps show rooms in buildings.

What else do maps show?

A Map Has Symbols

Symbols are pictures of objects.

You can draw a circle for a table.

You can draw a square for a desk.

What other symbols can you draw?

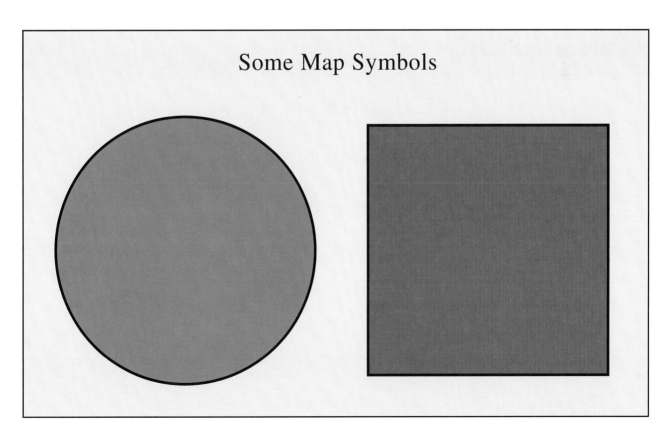

Some Map Symbols

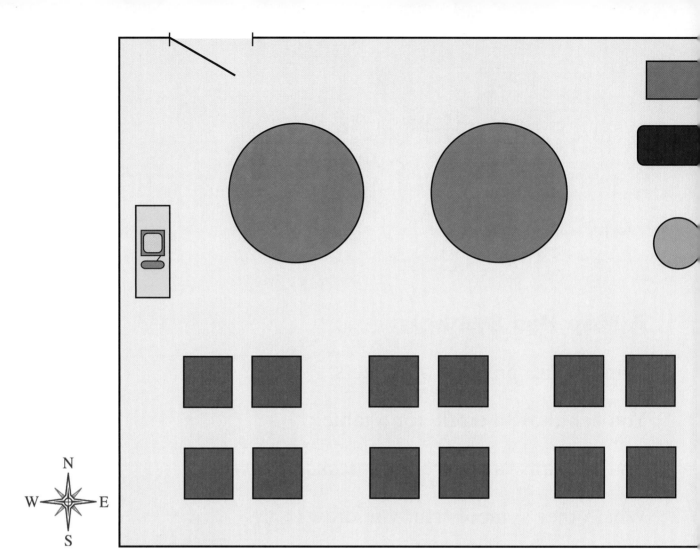

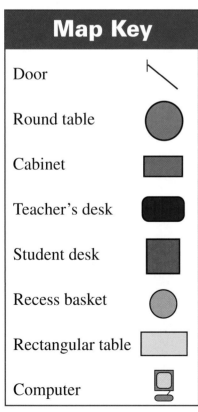

A Map Has a Key

A map key helps us read a map.

A map key shows each symbol.

Each symbol has a name.

Can you unlock the secrets of this

map?

A Map Shows Directions

We use letters to show direction.

We use N to mean north.

We use S to mean south.

What other directions can you name?

Wrap-Up

A map is a drawing of a place.

A map has symbols.

A map has a key.

A map shows directions.

What Was School Like Long Ago?

New Ideas

long ago

schoolhouse

hornbook

Schoolhouses Were Different

Long ago the schoolhouse was one room.

A stove was used for heat.

The teacher filled the stove with coal.

How is this different from your school?

Classrooms Were Different

One teacher taught everyone.

The younger children sat in front.

The older children sat in back.

How is this different from your classroom?

Children's Lives Were Different

Children walked a long way to school.

They played hoops at recess.

Naughty children wore a dunce cap.

How is this different from your life?

Classwork Was Different

Children used a hornbook.

A hornbook is a one-page book.

They wrote on slates with chalk.

How is this different from your classwork?

Wrap-Up

Schoolhouses were different.

Classrooms were different.

Children's lives were different.

Classwork was different.

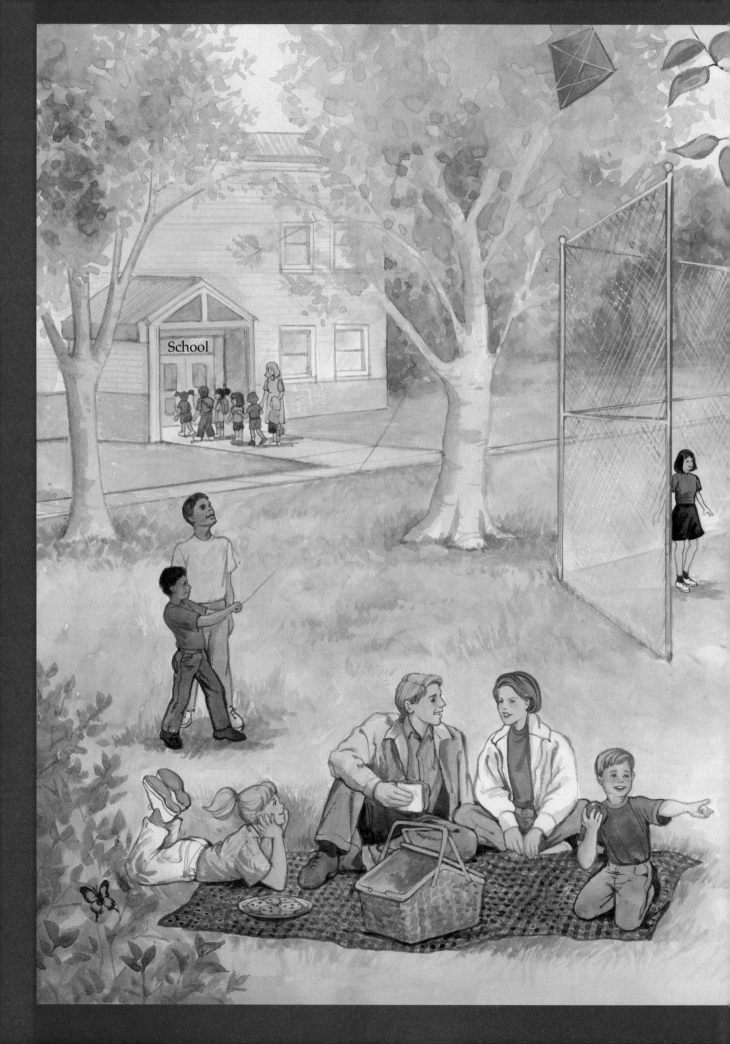

8

What Groups Do We Belong To?

New Ideas

school

family

community

We All Belong to Groups

A group has more than one person.

A group has something in common.

Groups can be big or small.

What groups can you name?

We Belong to School Groups

There are big and small groups at school.

Our school is a big group.

Our class is a smaller group.

What other groups do we have at school?

We Belong to Family Groups

Families can be big or small.

A family can be two people.

A family can be five people.

How many people are in your family?

48

We Belong to Community Groups

There are many kinds of groups.

Some groups play baseball.

Some groups share a religion.

What kinds of groups do you belong to?

Wrap-Up

We all belong to groups.

We belong to school groups.

We belong to family groups.

We belong to community groups.

How Are Families Special?

New Ideas

family members

homes

activities

Families Are Special in Different Ways

Families can be big or small.

They can live in the city or the country.

They like to do different things.

How is your family special?

Families Have Different Members

Some families have moms and dads.

Some families have brothers and sisters.

Some families have lots of cousins.

Who are the members of your family?

53

Families Live in Different Homes

Some families live in apartments.

Some families live in houses.

Some families live in mobile homes.

Where does your family live?

Families Like Different Activities

Some families like to picnic in the park.

Some families like to watch movies.

Some families like to go fishing together.

What does your family like to do?

Wrap-Up

Families are special in different ways.

Families have different members.

Families live in different homes.

Families like different activities.

What Do Families Need and Want?

New Ideas

need

want

Families Need Food

Families need food to live.

Food gives us energy.

Food helps us grow.

What foods does your family eat?

Families Need Clothing

Clothing keeps us warm and dry.

We wear hats in the summer.

We wear coats in the winter.

What kinds of clothing does your family wear?

Families Need Shelter

We all need a place to live.

A home gives us a safe place to be.

Shelter protects families from sun, wind,

rain, and snow.

What kinds of shelters do families live in?

Families Want Fun Things

Some families want new toys.

Some families want other fun things.

These fun things are called wants.

Wants are not things we need to stay alive.

What kinds of fun things might families want?

Wrap-Up

Families need food.

Families need clothing.

Families need shelter.

Families want fun things.

How Do Family Members Care for Each Other?

New Ideas

help with chores

share what you
know

spend time

Family Members Help Each Other

Families have chores to do.

Adults help by buying food.

Children help by washing dishes.

What chores do you do to help your family?

Family Members Share What They Know

Families talk and listen.

Adults teach children how to do new things.

Children share what they learn at school.

What will you share with your family today?

Family Members Show Their Feelings

Families care about each other.

Sometimes we show love with hugs and kisses.

Sometimes we use words to share our feelings.

How else do you show your family you care?

Family Members Spend Time Together

Families work together.

Families eat together.

Families play together.

What do you want to do with your family?

Wrap-Up

Family members help each other with chores.

Family members share what they know.

Family members show their feelings.

Family members spend time together.

How Do Families Change?

New Ideas

change

grow

move

Families Change Over Time

People change over time.

Families change when people change.

Can you think of one way your family

has changed?

Family Members Grow Older

People look different as they grow older.

They have different chores.

They can do more things.

What can you do now that you are older?

Families Grow Bigger

Families grow when people get married.

Families grow when children are born.

Some families grow by adopting people.

How many people are in your family?

Families Move to New Places

Sometimes families move to bigger homes.

Sometimes families need smaller homes.

Sometimes families want different homes.

Sometimes families move to new towns.

Wrap-Up

Families change over time.

Family members grow older.

Families grow bigger.

Families move to new places.

What Are Family Traditions?

New Ideas

tradition

celebrate

holiday

Traditions Are Special Ways of Doing Things

Some families eat special foods.

Some families wear special clothes.

What traditions does your family have?

Adults Teach Children

About Their Traditions

Some grandparents tell their

grandchildren special stories.

Some parents teach their children

special games.

Who teaches you about your

family traditions?

Families Celebrate Special Days in Different Ways

Some families celebrate birthdays with balloons.

Some families put up a piñata.

How does your family celebrate your birthday?

Families Celebrate Different Holidays

Some families celebrate Thanksgiving.

Some families celebrate the Chinese

Lantern Festival.

What special days can you name?

Wrap-Up

Traditions are special ways of doing things.

Adults teach children about their traditions.

Families celebrate special days in

different ways.

Families celebrate different holidays.

What Do Good Neighbors Do?

New Ideas

neighbor

next door

neighborhood

Neighbors Are the People Who Live and Work Near Us

Some neighbors live next door to us.

Some neighbors live down the street.

Some neighbors work in stores nearby.

Who are your neighbors?

Good Neighbors Help Each Other

Good neighbors do chores for someone who is sick.

Good neighbors teach younger kids how to play safely.

Good neighbors take care of each other's pets.

What do you do to help your neighbors?

Good Neighbors Get Along

Good neighbors wave when they see each other.

Good neighbors ask, "How are you?"

Good neighbors spend time together.

What do you do to get along with your

neighbors?

Good Neighbors Take Care of Their Neighborhood

Good neighbors put away their bikes.

Good neighbors keep their homes clean.

Good neighbors pick up trash.

How do you take care of your neighborhood?

Wrap-Up

Neighbors are the people who live and work near us.

Good neighbors help each other.

Good neighbors get along.

Good neighbors take care of their neighborhood.

Credits

Contents

(top to bottom) iv, A, DJ Simison; iv, B, DJ Simison; iv, C, Susan Jaekel; v, A, Gary Undercuffler; v, B, Jane McCreary; v, C, Renata Lohman; v, D, Len Ebert; vi, A, Carol Newsome; vi, B, Jane McCreary; vi, C, Susan Jaekel; vii, A, Susan Jaekel; vii, B, DJ Simison; vii, C, Dennis Hockerman; vii, D, Len Ebert

Chapter 1

2-3, DJ Simison; 4, upper, © 2002 Renzo Mancini/Getty Images/The Image Bank; 5, lower, Corbis; 6, upper, © 2002 Jim Cummins/Getty Images/FGP; 7, upper, © image100 Ltd

Chapter 2

8-9, DJ Simison; 12, upper, Corbis; 13, lower, Corbis

Chapter 3

14-15, Susan Jaekel; 16, upper, © Corbis Stock Market/Charles Gupton, 2002; 17, inset, © Corbis Stock Market/Mug Shots, 2002

Chapter 4

20-21, Gary Undercuffler; 23, upper, © 2002 Bruce Ayres/Getty Images/Stone; 24, lower, © 2002 Patti McConville/Getty Images/The Image Bank; 25, upper, © 2002 Michael Malyszko/Getty Images/FPG

Chapter 5

26-27, Jane McCreary; 29, lower, © 2002 Lawrence Migdale/Getty Images/Stone; 30, lower, © 2002 Ross Whitaker/Getty Images/The Image Bank

Chapter 6

32-33, Renata Lohman

Chapter 7

38-39, Len Ebert; 40, Corbis; 41, Corbis; 42, Corbis; 43, upper, Corbis

Chapter 8

44-45, Carol Newsome; 47, lower, © 2002 Genna Naccache/Getty Images/FPG; 48, upper, © 2002 Gary Buss/Getty Images/FPG; 49, upper, © 2002 Robert E Daemmrich/Getty Images/Stone

Chapter 9

50-51, Jane McCreary; 52, upper, © 2002 Tony Anderson/Getty Images/FPG; 53, lower, © 2002 Juan Silva/Getty Images/The Image Bank; 55, lower, Corbis

Chapter 10

56-57, Susan Jaekel; 58, upper, © 2002 Kevin Laubacher/Getty Images/FPG; 59, lower, Corbis; 61, © 2002 Ken Chernus/Getty Images/FPG

Chapter 11

62-63, Susan Jaekel; 64, © 2002 Elyse Lewin Studio Inc./Getty Images/The Image Bank; 66, © 2002 Jim Cummins/Getty Images/FPG; 67, © 2002 AJA Productions/Getty Images/The Image Bank

Chapter 12

68-69, DJ Simison; 70, © 2002 100% Rag Productions/Getty Images/FPG; 72, © 2002 Stephen Simpson/Getty Images/FPG; 73, © Corbis Stock Market/Ariel Skelley, 2002

Chapter 13

74-75, Dennis Hockerman; 76, © 2002 B. Tanaka/Getty Images/FPG; 77, © 2002 Paul Chesley/Getty Images/Stone; 78, upper, © 2002 Elyse Lewin Studio Inc./Getty Images/The Image Bank; 79, Corbis

Chapter 14

80-81, Len Ebert; **82,** © 2002 Bob Torrez
/Getty Images/Stone; **83,** © 2002 Don
Smetzer/Getty Images/Stone; **84,** © 2002
Brooklyn Productions/Getty Images/The
Image Bank; **85,** © 2002 Richard Price/Getty
Images/FPG